Still Life

Still Life

Gordon Hodgeon

STACK BOOKS

Published 2012 by
Smokestack Books
PO Box 408, Middlesbrough TS5 6WA
e-mail: info@smokestack-books.co.uk
www.smokestack-books.co.uk

Still Life
Gordon Hodgeon
Cover image: John Longstaff

Printed by
EPW Print & Design Ltd

ISBN 978-0-9571722-0-3

Smokestack Books is
represented by Inpress Ltd
www.inpressbooks.co.uk

In memory of Andrew Stibbs, who died December 2011.
He was my trusted friend and colleague over many years,
a brilliant teacher, a fine poet and a talented artist.

My thanks are due to family, friends and staff at The Hawthorns in Peterlee, who have helped me with my writing, particularly to Janet Graham, who helped me capture several poems in my head and move them onto paper, then later assisted me in editing the whole collection.

Acknowledgements are due to the editors of the following publications where some of these poems were first published: *English in Education*, Colette Bryce (ed) *Ink On Paper*; Andy Croft (ed) *Speaking English: Poems for John Lucas*; Richard Jemison (ed) *Teesway One Nine Nine*; Bob Beagrie and Andy Willoughby (eds) *The Wilds*.

r

Contents

This Bed

This bed is the bed of dreams, they all start
from this bed, a white hole swallowing
the collapsing star. They pulverise memory,
compound my tenses in a nightmare play.

This bed flies over the realities of day,
it ignores the world's exploding cries,
bedsides of sighs, of soft expiries,
the molten craters of birth.

This bed and me, we hovercraft,
we swish our skirts across
too numerous, too predictable agonies.
And you think I should care for them?

Even this bed sobs, gutters groan with tears,
the world a flash flood, cars elbowing bridges.
And tomorrow will bear down heavier,
will bend the earth's back.

We lie in wait for it, watching the sky,
never knowing what we must muddle through,
this night's throw of the diazepam dice.
As if, this bed and me, we were life's burden.

And down below us, sufferers making moan,
I hope you will sleep, every last one,
quiet and deep as the many dead,
with never a swift or little owl to wake you.

Man Writing an E-mail with his Carer

My room's at the end of the wing in the unit,
hers indeterminate, its window to the east.
Easy to move from here to the imagined there
of this postcard, from TV's clapping-happy hymn
through the wall, as deaf as any gospel choir
to argument, move to where she bends,
ink almost dry on her last word. That sideways light,
the chequerboard tiles, and hung behind her table
the dusky painting, its darkening oils.
The blackened frame bisects her world
between the fixed old dispensation
and shifting new, where paint is not quite dry,
anything could move, the dark fold in a skirt,
that cambric sleeve, a delicate lace cap.

The darkness is my hide, the sun out there
catches its fiery breath. My lines on screen
thicken and thin in crystal mist, carers change shifts
and busy in with medication, cups of tea, snatch glances
at summer through the glass, talk of a lottery win.
Pale wraiths of women lift the infant Moses,
Pharaoh's daughter, handmaidens, his deceiving mother.
There is the beginning of something,
a shiver in the gauze curtain, shadow of air,
the pale geometries of the window glass,
the maid at the still centre, arms crossed,
her gaze subdued, whatever stirs out there.
The light telling the hours. The woman writes,
her shoulders angled to the task.
One sheet of paper, all that is required.

Send for a new Vermeer to catch the silence,
the little window's light, my laptop's
scratched dull metal, the cheap pine desk,
the frame of the wheelchair, the carer beside me.
Watch as the distant leaves change bright for dim,
shadows relax on lawns, walkers on the unseen path
go home. Nothing amazes like the garden we have lost,
the naked baby before us, the severity of each moment,
errors folded, unfolded. The words not sent, not spoken.

Visitor

You bent down by my side,
leaned on the arm of the settee
where three of us sat. Three of fifteen
in the day lounge. You are most kind.
Got a dropped, half-chewed sweet
on your trousers to remember that.
Where I have ended up.
Days and nights lost at sea.

This is *Safehaven*
where the tides push us all.
We gasp on the dry land,
stagger up and down on it,
write messages in it for angels.
Wings outstretched, they can't stop now.

I am hankering after home,
slippery on the tongue,
I howl it like an abandoned dog: ho o ome.
Do you think I have become a child?
Some home, some dog's home,
the address keeps changing.
Am I a pup now? Are you my mother,
all teats, all tongue? But she would not be crying.

You look out of the window
for magpies or the undertaker,
something to amuse me.
Pass the parcel slowly till the claw
shows through to lift me to heaven.
You would like to believe it.

Every night I am kept here
you come and go, my flying island
that's you, and where do you go?
To my lawn's moss? To the outmost star?

Somehow you return. I think you
drive over a cliff somewhere, you land
in a flashing-blue-light box.
What do you come for? I am dying.
You can't croon me up from here,
I can't tail you out, my lyre-bird.
We know that, we don't like to mention.

I'm out in front on this one. Like a god
I put in meaning or extract it.
This habit of yours, this care for me
so old that it dies hard, what if you
cracked its case open and the wind blew?
What if it did not matter?

My cup spills over. Almost always.
Tea, soup, milk slops down chin, neck, shirt.
Full of days and their wide-eyed shadows.
What was hunger is my tray on time.
This thirst is baked on hell's hot cinders.
It would breathe fire if I had breath.

You've stopped trying the brightness.
I keep you waiting.
We'll be parted as soon as sorrow,
anything we say taken down,
useless, bent wheels dropped in the pit.

Save your vows for another day.
Let the waste in, let it trickle in
tendril by tendril, inquiring if
the space is available or might
be available, might it wait…
and tell it what I said.

Last words, soon enough forgot,
need strength I don't have.
No more flap out into air.
Hymn. Curtains. Off we go.
No applause in this case.

North Tees Epiphany

Up in the ship of warming air
I see earth roll, unroll ten miles or more
to the grey invisible sea, through terraces,
playgrounds, shops, car parks, wasted spaces.

The bridge an extinct spider, a clutch of long-cooled
towers, the low-lit clouds appalled
at the ruin of river, its nuclear cup
that must not be spilled, the whole brave balls-up.

This is where we live and if, we say if,
this airship, its skilful crew, deliver us safe
through the dream of our needful pain,
it's where we'll be glad to go home.

Always the engines' thrum as gulls weave
wind's fabric round and *Save us, save us*
their window-baffled, hardly-hoping call.
I am one ear of many, one eyeball.

Big ship's the grand, the theatrical show,
staging nativities three floors below
while this top deck sets tragicomic bones,
our breaks, distortions, fractures, agony.

Assorted healing heap, this ossuary soars
over the silenced houses, children, cars,
over the floodplain, over the ferny moor.
An hour to wait now for our visitors.

These faithful all will come, arise, adore
the new-born, the last-chancers, every floor,
will bring us frankincense and myrrh and gold
from down below, from out there's dark and cold.

Natural History

The dinosaur's all beams and rafters
in the bleached arch of its spine,
knotted and lumpy beyond ancient oak,
a bone-house baked in fossil stone.

And our two kids still arguing
all those years in the museum.
Could it be real? Was it a fake?
It is always time to go home.

My own backbone got no attention,
a lost relation of *triceratops*,
ghosting me, always a step behind,
shadow to standing starts and stops.

I dragged around this rucksack just in case,
a frame inside a flappy canvas skin
transported by the busy legs beneath,
an afterthought, I thought, of evolution.

Or it would bend to sky's unbending gaze
the ripple of a cyclist's bony spurs
in rainbow gortex visibility
between the saddle and the handlebars.

But over sixty years or so it seems
the weight of weight clamped in the vertical
squeezed disks together in a vice,
strangling the disregarded nerves' canal.

Now legs are left to dangle legless down
and struggle inching through each inch of plod,
the forward/backward/sideways shunts
my brain would manage if it only could.

The surgeons promise me that they will try
titanium. A rod or two might save
me from my frequent falls from grace,
redeem old fault lines from an early grave.

I hope they're right and, yes, I'll let you know
if they restore me to an upright stance,
swapping the dinosaur's demise
for leggy humankind's pretence.

Or kids can dispute if I'm fake or real,
the specimen that one day will be shown
in natural history's marble halls:
screwed space-age metal and primeval bone.

Lessons, August 2008

Of learning not to walk: the trekking pole
recalls old chapel prints, the lathered score
of lambs Good Shepherd stirs with golden crook,
bright ether, Menwith Hill excrescence. Or

a frost-lipped Capt'n Oates or such good chap
loping slowmotioned into snow's machine. The grim
down-stabbing of the rubber tip, the legs
sea-swaying on the spinal drop they swing from

while helpless has-beens watch from dusty frames,
lost demi-gods: maybe they got TV, this on it,
scratched image in old film stock, ghastly joke
from some disastrous newsreel best forgot.

Never forget, you will - and here we go again -
the funny walk, the fist against the wall, the perilous
footfalling up the stairs, the bliss of shopping trolleys,
the can-you-can't-you board each train or bus.

Might someday face-to-face the ones who know
all ruined battlements and crumpled zones,
who write the runes now, wield their laser knives,
who're quick to scrape out all our crumbling bones.

So hobble, heroes, on board song or story,
see Doctors Who will bless the firmament
and frogmarch us into our last sunset.
Time Lords dismiss us? Piss in their Tardis tent.

Flog It

Pack me down and out of
The Antiques Roadshow
to *Cash in the Cellar*:
experts, don't you worry,
shake your many heads:
'The key's condition, sorry, so
please wheel him off in his rusty barrow.'

And it's on a Sunday morning
at the Sellafield Bygones Fair,
on a fold-down operating table.
I'm a shivering junkie
in medias res, a brassed-off monkey
grinning like a Blair,
glowing in the rubble.

Bargain-hunter-gatherers,
faces like stale bread,
scuttle lithe as cockroaches
over the lino.
A fiver for me, a bite or a bean? No.
I'm nearly, almost,
might as well be, dead.

My minders won't enjoy this
jumble sale wail.
No room in the bin,
no hymn in the boot,
everything must go and make some loot.
The land is filled in
every leaky hole.

Away to the warehouse
of bankrupt stock,
flood-damaged Noah bathmats *et omnibus*.
It's warm enough and dry, they
won't kick up a fuss
if you leave them in the dark
and double-lock the lock.

Come back in the morning,
now the sale can start,
but you won't find me. Just
don't give a stuff,
a fart or a fistful of love. I'm off,
off to the incinerator
on a rare handcart.

Of the Tree

We are the broken branches of the tree,
each named a mimic of the living woods:
Ash, Beech, Oak, Poplar, Holly.
Over dejected, splintered heads
the leaves rush, shiver, never tired,
but we're unfit for any timber yard,
the warped, split, twisted, nearly dead
assembly for the earthy underworld.

Each a fixed fragment of the maypole dance,
all of us incomplete complete the set:
a lost leg; missing hand; eyes, ears *sans*
sight, *sans* hearing; shaking or swollen feet.
Our stepping song is *Rehabilitate*
for we are meant to grow again, to rise
up from our wheelchairs, from this supine state,
put out fresh green, shake fists at gloomy skies.

Days will discover; this one's curve of brass
marches green-veined light and shadow
over the quivering measures of the grass.
Seeming fast, slow, the evanescent now.
Then sun's set, birds still: early tomorrow
we will expect them up for song and shine.
And why not raise a glass or fallen bough
with sap substantial as communion wine?

Thank You, Jelly

I am making a hymn,
a praise song for this body,
which floats inert
down from my brain.

I want to thank it, this shivering blancmange,
this paralysed jellyfish, for all it has done
these past seventy years.
It has given my mouth so many meals,
it has shifted me over many miles,
it has made love for me, run itself out of breath,
it has undergone surgeries to keep me alive.
I cannot put a number on all its services.

Now it trembles at each whim
of the tide, alert to all sensation,
but has lost its sting.
Only my voice can shock you, electrify.
So I am helpless, but still
a trifle dangerous.

Housebound

You get a sense of what it's like to lie
alone and in the earth, set to decay.
The regulars will visit hallowed ground,
a few old friends include you in their rounds
from time to time, but most will let you rot,
forgetting they already have forgot.
Of course we can't know that for certain sure,
but some were coming and have missed the door,
while others phoned or emailed, sent a card
and, duty done, went shopping or abroad.
A few more didn't ask or realise
you'd disappeared from view. Whatever lies
beyond horizons can't be their concern,
they live for what's in range, don't seem to learn
what lurks outside their urn-shaped biscuit box
where sweets compacted lie, day's paradox:
it's not all-things, though beautiful and bright,
inevitably swallowed up by night.
Well, I might rattle on like this some time,
preferring home-grown groans to the sublime
of poetry, art, music, friendship, love.
Fact is, out there or, my conceit, above,
are many folk who care for me, who worry
about, pray for, want to help, will scurry
over if I call and ask. They'd lift me if they could
out of the grave, at least out of the mud
I have to blunder through just now. They can't
and that's the sod of what is most sincerely meant
but does not work, which makes me curse and blame
my well-wishers, for whom I'd do the same
if our roles were reversed, me up, them down.
Send them a card or flowers, a *Get Well Soon*.

Awake

The late-night film, old Bertolucci's *Dreamers*,
his only company, she as usual absent,
the cocktail of music, sex, cinema
nevertheless enough. He'll reinvent
what she told and might well not have told him
about the sixties, revolution, Paris,
lovers gone missing. From this merry mayhem
the long loop back to home and him she married.

Kept in that present like a dusty wreath,
he knows the argument still rakes her head
with how she could break out, might make the truth
just fit the day. *Dans la rue!* Knows how instead
she's grown slow compensations *sans merci:*
gardens, grandchildren. For better and for worse.

Easter in ICU

It is my body on this slab of bed
with one white sheet my cover.
No angels at my foot or head,
but nurses here, who hover:
they lift me, turn me over.

Their ritual attentions stalk
across this tomb, deep day, deep night.
My head rings with their echoed talk
of all that's wrong, should be put right.
I wish these suns were not so bright.

The surgeon has no plan to raise
me from the dead I imitate,
no flicker in his weary face
gives hope that I might levitate,
ascend to a more gracious state.

The nurses seek out breaks in skin
where bed-sore fiends can root and stretch,
while, like a roasting hog, my grin
turns on the spit, poor naked wretch.
Stripped bare, the bones are for the ditch.

Instead, let me be hoist aloft,
sole claimant to that bleak Cross Fell,
wind-broken bracken, peat sink-soft,
the weathershed of heaven and hell
where hikers' boots imprint like nails.

Chicken Legs

after Richard Slee, *Chicken Legs 2005*

Skip the jokes these are not
useful prosthetics cold
oily yellows and veined pinks.

My dad took one and a bit legs
to the grave, the rest was trashed
in a hospital incinerator.

Frank Bird's factory's enough
for a million chicken lives
we eat some at the barbeque.

The smoothed-off stump got sores
in its laced-up leather pouch
tried all sorts, not much use.

You could juggle these thighs
in a ballet of chicken legs
or drop to smithereens.

He walked with a click, a click
that locked the joint
took his weight the next yard.

You stand here, weigh them up
like Marks and Spencers
free-range big value packs.

Don't their birds have good lives
and he couldn't dance OK
but got around click click.

Long division sums
one flesh, fragmented trajectories
the awkwardness of resurrection.

Some rich Medici kept
a saint's bone in a golden box
you can believe in chicken legs.

At the Window

Here I have watched
these trees grow large
and wide, the five
the space allowed,
that with each year
carry a greater weight
of branch and leaf,
blossom and fruit.

They make my plot content,
their unrelenting lack
of second thought
about expansion, height,
assuages growing pains.

Now in mid-May
they scatter drops of shade
over the mossy grass
that needs another cut
and over older man
who planted it and them
thirty-odd years ago.
He never dreamed
we'd still be here,
garden and gardener.

The children up and gone,
fencing renewed,
neighbours removed or died,
the most solid timber
split down with lightning,
which will strike again,
or storm or novel flood
sweep us to bonfires.

Today the earliest roses bud
beyond this window glass
the trees obscure.

The Leaving

for Julia

Taking my leave of you, the house, garden
where we grew three children,
was it that we had outstayed
our welcome or that, just tired,
this place needed a change of voices?

Though you had left some days before,
taken into care, which I could not provide.
Now my turn, the ambulance to a bare bed
and still more surgery. I never made it back
so you'd to stay away.
The house was emptied, up for sale,
our children's labours.
Trees lopped, hedging sheared, heating turned down low.

And all that said, four seasons
have gone their way,
my sense of sky's become
the emulsioned white of ceiling,
of sun, the ornate hung circle
of a shaded bulb,
my garden is cut flowers in water.

Winter hardened everything, hawthorn and pyracantha
lost their berries, all bare sticks, sharp scratches.
By the garden window, that first green thrust,
tight fist of snowdrops bides its time,
will soon enough surprise new watchers
with its hard, pale pearls.

One day I came to see you, my wheelchair
strapped in the minibus, nurse by my side.
They placed us wheel by wheel,
steady as Moore's king and queen
on their Scottish hillside. We stayed two minutes
till my breathing blocked and I was rushed

to the hospital, leaving you bereft.
It was a tearing apart,
the last leaf sucked from the wood,
ripping its fingernails.

And now there are new owners,
making the house their own.
Peter from next door telling me this,
first project, a room for their one-year-old.
I think they will clear the garden
for the child's first steps,
for balls to roll and bounce.

Under the grass, weak as worm castings,
our weary archaeology, the bones of buried animals:
one pheasant hit on the Sunday morning run
to the swimming pool; one rabbit banned from your school
which would not dig its way out again.
Also, the procession of cats stalking through childhoods.

So next your turn to visit me,
our daughter driving, your carer by your side.
We did some talking this time, but dear me,
your anxious mind began its litany
of questions: is it time to go now?
And repetitions, till we set you free
to make your safe way home.
Yet it was not your home.

Here, in the early hours
I often wake, hear the comfort,
your regular breath beside me.
But this is a single bed
and the breath I hear is the ventilator
filling and emptying my lungs.

April

for Libby at seven weeks old

I met this new-born under April sun
where the year's days lengthen,
stretch limbs to the warmth.
She a few hours short of seven weeks,
me few days short of seventy years.

For her everything is new,
she is new herself,
every face, every voice
fits to her understanding,
each tissue of response.
And here I lie, my old thinking,
we have seen and heard all there is.

Then her mother, my daughter,
lays her against my shoulder.
And warm against my cheek
her breathing slows
and eyes drift down to sleep.

Libby

at 12 weeks old

It's you up there, examines my old face,
spies something you can catch,
glimmers in the dark down here.
You cast a line of sensibility
which lures me, reels me in.
I watch your ancient, oceanic grin
shape for me, toothless and rounded.

Before you slip away, little fish,
dance of your fish-bright eyes,
sing me that song again:
ah…ah…ah…mm.
Fish, dolphin, mermaid, whale,
the music's baffling, beautiful.
In at the deep beginning, here
I learn to swim, love you for it.
We are in our element.

VE Day

War baby, toddler, fifty summers on,
I show my kids this battered photograph,

the VE Party in our safe back street,
its trestle-tops and grown-ups all pulled down.

The satellites watch over and sing silence,
saucers are fixed to catch the falling sky.

The shelter where we huddled under air-raids
is flattened lawn, bright as a victory jelly.

I name the dead, find out of focus
at the back, wearing his trilby, dad.

Kids at these tables ate to the future,
to hands across free Europe, to the sunny side.

Always keep a camera ready, where the light
might grow or fail, for such a picture.

Promenade

after Horace

Now all you girls who kissed me when a lad
are like me, pensioned off, your time's been had,
and, if we met, we wouldn't recognise
each other's bodies, faces, years' disguise.
We'd walk right past the lips, the looks, the limbs
we'd dream about while singing the same hymns,
be put off scent by tweed coat, sheepskin mitts,
and not sniff out the perfumed smelly bits
incarcerated in hot nylon mesh,
be comforted by well-known spreading flesh.
My creaking sweethearts, you could teach some charm
to half-dressed totty tottering through Yarm
as if the cattle-market still existed.
I still admire the kind way you resisted
us clumsy boys' testosteronic gropes,
your patience as you taught us stronger ropes
of human love seeking a lifelong mate:
you knew that flowers had a fade-by date.
But did you find him you were looking for
or have you squandered sex on some dull bore
instead of chancing one wild fling with me?
Just think about it, as you make his tea.

Glazebury Girl

Dark nights,
I met you on the steps down from The Tech,
your night-school class. From here
slow to the bus station,
last one for your journey home.
We dragged along the cindered backs
of Railway Road, pressing our weight
on damp yard walls, dank gates.
Under your watch-bright eyes
I learned the give and the resist
of lips, kissed, kissing,
while untaught hands quite failed
to make their way inside your winter coat,
its fingered tufts and curls of bluey-grey.

Summer was different,
gave no hour to hide.
We traipsed the pavements
by the East Lancs Road
or trailed the edges of flat, stubbly fields
which spread out from the village-string
of houses, farms, your chapel and the church,
dark stone against your family's cottage,
old apple trees shading your garden.

Invited there for solid Sunday teas,
triggering my dad's repeated joke
about your place: did you have
apple pie sandwiches? I never did,
that awkward, Brylcreemed lad,
soon to go off to university,
you'd taken up with at a Social
with Buffet or a Pie and Peas,
some chapel in the Circuit raising funds.

Those two young Methodists
all arms and legs, remembering each dance
learned painfully and now required.
First words exchanged, first glances held,
while cautious purses kept their change
for soft drinks and the bus fares home.

And what's become of them, of us,
it's hard to say, hard to write down
as fifty years and some have scratched
and scraped this page of mine.
What I have gleaned is this:
we are both still alive, but are grown separate,
as bolder loves and life-meant marriages,
as children's births and parents' deaths,
as faith kept seasonal through all the years
with ploughshare, seed-cast, reap and store,
or slowly set aside, all bramble-snagged,
have us quite prised apart,
unnoticed as the deep tectonic plates
nudging these northern plains and Pennine hills.

But I would like to know,
when all I know will soon be ignorance,
whether you still put trust
in that belief we shared in Harvest Home
before we had to reckon with
what all our days have brought us.
Perhaps God knows I tried, but years
wore down, wore through, the fabric tore.
At the back-end, I can't accept one Word
Incarnate, even as my flesh fails.
I might require salvation, but it wouldn't work,
cliff-hanger snatch out of the fiery pit,
Hell's teeth, jaws I don't think exist.

Back then, back there, we were child soldiers,
sunbeams in smoky air that Jesus wanted.
Polished and drilled in Sunday School,
knowing those hymns by heart,
we marched, we shone,
paraded our new clothes, bright as the banners,
in step with hired brass bands from pits and factories,
those Whitsun Walks that haunt forgetful streets.

And all of that's as far away
as you are now from me. I'm left
with distance and small mercies,
whoever gives, however given,
that I still count like blessings:
grandchildren's kisses, glimpses of poems,
the studied breath of the ventilator,
light through the curtains, learning to be content
with each day's mortal measure.

If you have stayed God-fearing, which I guess,
and full of expectation for the life to come,
I'll pray, for once, you'll share it with your own good sort,
kind Glazebury Methodists who make no fuss,
and not with clumsy-clever-clogs like me.
I really was one then, lacking the grace
to thank you for the love you showed
my dad, crippled, stuck in the Infirmary.
He kept on telling me how good you were,
lovely, but I kept sullen silence.
You and me, we'd finished, hadn't we?
And off I went again that hundred miles or more
up hill and down and far away to bury
head in books, mind in all those words.

So here I sit, have little left to say,
locked in this wheelchair's pew-hard seat.
Too many years gone, I can't face you now.
More miles, more hills than I will ever make.

From Cross Fell

Hardly the roof of the world
scraping at sky that thin.
More of a lean of leaky sheds,
a grey-green tarpaulin
hauled over, weighted down.

Water in flashes. Walls of stone.
The broken drainpipe path
up to this guttery ridge
can hatch out little eggs of blood
with grasses' wiry scratch.

From here down rain makes tracks
to seas each hand can reach:
close Eden's swampy tribe,
Tees by its high-dive foss,
the eely strands of Tyne.

Their floodlights fatten up,
fill in the long yards' cracks.

Long Meg

A campervan by the prehistoric stones:
dusk already, glad to be out of the field
and through the gate, I know the metalled road
from here to home but, still to be passed through
as I come nearer, the boulders in the ring
thicken like knots, make a noose round me.

Last of the sun backlights Blencathra,
great stranded whale on that luminous shore,
when I see the woman pacing and talking.
She shudders as I call across. The tall stone
and old oaks reach out fingers of darkness.
She wants to camp, the sign says No Camping.

She's dented the van's rear wing. On that low stone.
Reversing. Just when she needs to sell it.
Time she was back down under. For the hip op.
The van's not damaged much, fit for the breaker's.
I tell her there's a campsite three miles off;
she will not, she says, use campsites, needs nothing.

Or she could try at Melmerby, the green
travellers use after the Fair, she'd be fine
and the pub has good food. You go this way.
She will see. Don't leave it long, I say, night falls
faster now, sense it falling behind me.
Time I was away. I walk my last mile.

The road she should take. Cottage dark as walls
of a prison I taught in years ago,
been back in dreams inside. This night I've a key.
Nothing goes past my shadow down the lane.
Soon it's dawn, chaffies invent old curses,
do battle with the blue tits for the feeders.

I bike to the shop, bread and the paper,
the green's empty. Next to the daughters' circle
and the great stone chisel plunged into earth
where the light said to itself 'Stab, stab here!'
I see sheep in the ring, two crow-feathers
tied to swing from an oak.

Up Hartside

An unlicked lolly for the thirsting sun,
my bald head bares its skin of ice-thin blush
starting to melt down the wet stick of neck.

Flashback to – cycling all the way up, sprawled
now at the head of the pass. Just sky, lapwing,
three gulls, the bench outside the Hartside Cafe.

Can't get enough, that old prune sun,
so tantalised, can't drink, can hardly sip
with those several septic tongues.

The rasp of them on the grain of scalp
lifting the beads of my sweat,
rubbing each moist pore open.

No modest shadows, pushy as vampire's lip,
sun's leery bloodied eye marks me as ripe,
at my eat-by date, bends to its fangy bite,

will force its poison in if not prevented.
Scan the hills, the haze of Solway. No microlite,
no leathered rescue corkscrewing road and plot.

I'm to be saved nevertheless up Hartside top
by snap of Blackpool sands from fifty years,
the knotted hankie on my long-dead baldy dad.

So suck you, red-eye, draculaic sun
up there in your slavering castle.
Look where the upstart cyclists snake the pass,

their knotted banners red as shampoo'n'set
you'll get in the Irish Sea. Mine's loose over the neck,
O'Toole like, pinned with my UV shades.

To Long Meg

We often walk up there; the hill is steeper
than at first, ten years ago; a new gate
by the cattle-grid, an iron hasp
that fills my hand. The laneside hedges
much as they were, the red soil banking under them
a shifting tracery of rabbit-holes. Every year
spirits of curlew, hare and sacrificial field beasts
love and lament their timely incarnations.

At the top field visitors halt. The road
runs through into a farmyard, the footpath
swings to the right, four pastures to the church.
In the top field we hold, caught in the swirl,
the cast net of the stones, sharing their orb
with maybe ten cows, three clambering children,
one man with a table and two girls dancing.
A busy day that would be, mostly the two of us.

We've learned to thread these earth-beads
on our walking string, move to the knot-point,
the sandstone pendant heavy in air,
horizons' eyes on us. I will explain to newcomers
the bunkum of Tudor myths, the witchcraft hokey.
You might note that the light fades, autumn comes on.
We count the stones again which never dance,
chalk off the numbers of shared solstices.

Reds

Our tutor ends his sentence
and clicks the stereo.
Across two centuries of night
Viennese evening shivers out its stars
of candle-light from speakers,
high in corners, into late morning
here, a Saturday in snowdrop time.
And here dead lovers dance their swirls,
piano, violin, a shadowed ecstasy.

Last hundred years and more
the Himalayan cedar's swell
has washed its slow green tide
over this room's tall window.
Behind us, where we sit all ears,
Skiddaw is huddled, gagged and bound,
thick ropes of cloud waiting to fray to snow.

Beside, in cedar's even heavier shade,
a rough-logged feeding-table, could be larch.
A neighbour in the weekend student rows,
she has been here before, elucidates:
'Red squirrels. Watch the cedar tree.'

Music that flickers, slowly fades.
The darkening room,
mind taking its sad leave.
A silence presses
from the silent hill.

And now I see them:
one, then two, then three
as light as snowflakes
dropping their soft flares
from dimming corners of the cedar sky.
They scatter out their runs of flame,
the precious ink along the staves,
turn a pale day to this bright-breathed-on fire.

Life Class

with a group of artists and writers

We are arranged, the four sides of a rectangle
its cracked edges these square work-tables
tops of scabby teak, others scuffed mustard.
Light is diffused through windows, higher cloud
sifting the rays, shadowing the bursts of rain.

Our model floats above the surface of floorboards
would polish back to oak, our model is laid out
on her lilo, old cushions from a lost settee
easy in private pool, the slightest breath
lifting her belly, fronds of her fingers stirring.
Dark weed hair falls into textures of cloth
clings in a moss where her legs part
from where they flow in their echoing lines.
The horizon of skull, the pencil stroke of eyebrow
the delicate fringe of one lid shivering
finer than any brush here, thinner than trembling lines.
The soul looks out, timid bright, from its hard shell.

Given how you lie and where I sit today
our model, your face is set away from me
in the gentle slope of a hill, its rise and fall
with, where men took stone, the flickering tarn of the eye.
And the wolds of your body slope up and away
not an abruptness, the angles camera might configure,
nor the abstractions of clothing. It is not
as an ideal either you are come here, but one
holding-together, while the glue's strong, the human genome
in a warming of sun, a conspiring of waters,
afternoon in the studio, from the life everlasting.

Along four edges, on the worn tiles of the tables
the writers bend to their ant trails crossing, re-crossing,
the artists intent on the scrape cries of charcoal.
Their creatures spring from your body and at once
are changing as you are, your indecipherable
nanosecond modulations, the reality of image,
the accretion of lines, the gathering of shadows,
our hands winding the sun through the sky
into a final darkness where, this same afternoon,
in mortuaries, quick dug graves, bulldozed in-fills,
the murdered lie unpuzzled under dry heaven.

Gentle-voiced man on his bed, one leg a pointing stump,
told me through camera and translator
'Bombs are not simple.' An expert followed with
the cluster's artistry, the swarms of copper bees.
They are too many to count, the war is over
as a heavy shower rattles the studio window,
simple enough, adjusts the wash of light
on your ribs and thigh, unwounded, whole,
our model. You after all may be
impossible, hologram of the maker's intention.
Young as you are, how else survived unscathed?

Design, target, trajectory: elements of purpose
exact as choice of brush, plain as one just word.
Galleries where time's to kill. I was never here
before, the poolside of your nakedness
our model. I am getting a glimmer of
this obstinacy of eyes and fingers,
their marks on paper, what they will lift from you.
Some understanding how we are small,
ephemeral, wavering in the light, plain lovely,
how we might celebrate earth made flesh
while we are.

From John's Life Sketch

for John Longstaff

To see ghosts and without belief
in the wash of this grey-white

where, drooping bergs of ice,
the windows loom. Wetness of light

on green skeins of fog-flesh
shiver inked lines of bone.

Here is the statue, the solid
marble meat of her, the sheaf

of one hand's fingers harvested
in coral, its lament

for the day she was split
out of the belly of rock

chiselled into beauty.
And this bed, made for her.

Tall Ships in the Shipley

The frantic to-and-from of skies and seas
gives painters work, makes space in galleries.

Ships heave, decks twitch, masts lean in wedding dress,
brave elements with their newfangledness.

So with their brushes, lenses, box of tricks
artists shift air and wet into this fix.

They frame it in gilt wood, add title to it:
'Coast Scene', 'Bound Homeward', 'Coming Into Port'.

Each ship's an island, risking liberty,
dragging day-trippers out of their depth like me.

Dry ground's illusion, landmarks swept away,
imagination washes feet of clay.

The parquet floors swell with the pregnant moon,
the granite creaks, the ceiling trickles down.

Extractor fans break out in harsh gull cries,
horizons leap and lurch before my eyes.

Gateshead's good ship laden with precious ore
lurches land-lover wisely back to shore.

Bella Pateman For This Night Only

after Frank Sutcliffe, *Boardie Willie* (Whitby, 1890s)

A cart is crossing the bridge that's swung
across the sun-slapped harbour, the rippled bowl.
The drink licks shadows on the crusting steps.

This sandwich man is tossed into the tides,
bait for desires sharp for the salty sea,
must lure their pennies to his siren's song.

The dog-end job's transformed by clever Frank,
an arty joke the better class would buy,
still do: the battered cod of face is mocking hers

which is pre-Raphaelite and thorny-crowned.
Pain passed, my pen will write her face's lines,
who might have watched that snatcher flash his tricks.

She might have jumped at Scarborough last night
after the show's slow hand-claps, boozy boos,
the run-out sands of emptying stalls.

Here staring from the glass are his gaunt chops
and her young ghost. The box with the hood
and its headless man have snapped them up

as a gull gulps fish-heads. Have done away with
their souls. Done away with the moment of death.
The clicking guillotine bites neck, fixes us all.

Sailor's Song

Off Anglers' Island, Angel Strand,
the names as shifty as the tides,
we watched the seals play, years gone by,
inhaled the wrinkle-nose of weed,
scrunched frothy pebbles down the sand.

The salt of lost love twists my jaw
as you watch out that fearful surge,
a whip for the seals in its swerve and thrash.
But why do you stand on the harbour edge
washed pale by the crash and the gnaw?

Dried-up ink in my dry-land pen,
the blood-seep from my heart all bled,
the sea swells up to a bruising lip
and it kisses a beach hut, licks it aboard,
a box to dress a drowned sailor in.

And all I've left is a gap-toothed song,
you teetering there at the dancing crest,
your hair flung back like a comet's is
on its long dive down to the fiery feast
where wheat is as chaff and right as wrong.

I should haul you safe in under a wing,
hold you as close as the words we spoke.
But it's well that you take this cold embrace
on your silky pelt and swim or choke
round-eyed, electric, remembering.

Moors Meeting

Moor must have been all at sea, his boat
battered, him shipwrecked, not first, not last
under these hanging headlands,
far from Venice, out of harm's way,
but that was elsewhere, later, how shall I put it?
In a play.

More also must have come here astray
from his usual habitat, not in my view
a pilgrim rambling to his fled utopia,
nor on the run from that strong tower's hold,
where we hope he might have dreamed this different field
of cloth of gold.

Unlikely, yet my claim's that they met on this bold
ridge of heather and bracken, by this scope
of sky, looked at that scour of tides that shivers
this island's skeleton, bites at an older plot
than either fell prey to, and talked an hour
on this very spot.

Moor never was good at the future, More, though not
inclined to unreason, was more so and stated
in learned Italian that he for his part could be content,
after losing his head, to return as a curlew or lapwing,
to coast over just such a stretch of perfection
and only sing.

'Tommy, you English altar-boys, all the same!', that sting
in the voice, slight hint at the twist of love to hurt
(as we said, that came later), replied the general,
'Life all books and brinkmanship, death's slate washed clean as this!'
noting the wind at his face, the shimmer of light
on a land at peace.

Well, believe us or not, time came to dismiss
Moor and More from this and every high place
and they walked to the ends of their paths, as we must,
leaving stones and the sheep and each hidden spout
born again in new eyes, with, worn on new skin, the bright dark
jewelling of jet.

Identifications

Hamstead Colliery, March 1908

Which were brought out of the pit

eleven lying in a group in three rows
on their faces, side by side
one on top of the road
one on Wednesday near no.19 Cross Road
two on Friday in no.1 East Road
next day another, one more on Sunday
the last the Friday following

John Jones, collier – Ernest, younger brother
recognised the features
Thomas Summerfield – his three sons
Charles by his boots, John by his clogs, Walter by his shirt
Reuben Burton – his son, Enoch
by the description of his flannel band
also George Warner, collier – Enoch Burton
his flannel belt, his baldness
Wilfred Lawley – his brother, William
by his widow's (very ill, suffering now from fits)
description of his clothing
unable to recognise the features
Sophia Mitchell – husband, Samuel
his pipe, his knife, various articles
Fanny Bradley, widow of James
by means of his watch and chain and his bottle
Mrs Hancock, widow of James, last to be recovered
by means of a piece of cloth and a sock

Mrs Jones, Canal Road – twice married
her first husband
killed in the pit eleven years ago
four children by her second
their ages 6, 4, 3 and 2
him crippled in the pit two years ago
will never work again –

has lost her son, Joseph, breadwinner
the girl, 11, is crippled
the girl of 4 has a wasted leg
the girl of 3 has deformed limbs

verdict returned of 'accidental death'

Large Winged Vessel

after Colin Pearson, *Large Winged Vessel, 1982*

You found me six feet down
trowels itching for skin:
two chipped curves of bone
brushed clean, out into sun.

Revealed this baked clay ring
from the dirt, remembered song
of an evil time, blew my strong
horn, each bruised bone a wing.

In air I squat, in light, coiled heavy
as heaviest artillery,
immune and monstrous bee,
thick-set on slaughter: 'What I do is me.'

Will winged vessel fly or speak,
bleed for you? You might break
my silence, prove your scholastic
cunning, get your frost to crack

glazed hide where no nerve lives.
It is not that I am brave
to withstand you, not that I love
death. I was born to this in the hive.

Courses

The antique city is deep in its walls,
over its ground and over my head,
under the soil of the gardens, under
the worn feet of its pavements,
drowned in the sediment of centuries,
mislaid in foundations of so much ruin.

Today they just lounge here, white and cold,
lit like clouds in this blue autumn.
I've also seen them wet and grey
as men my age in our bathhouses.
They muffle up at nights, these ghosts
of my passages, the crushing stone
Commendatores trucking in to dine
on anyone who dares to scrawl *Fuck off!*

Still I should kick against the bruisers,
enough of their stiff lips, backdrops and props
for bloody histories, blind turn-your-blocks
on slaughters, executions, martyrs.
I repent my indulgence of lovely walls,
which offered no shelter, built no barricade.

No doubt the upstanding amongst them
shine as bright in hypocrisy as, dear Lord,
the upstanding amongst us, denizens
of rotten boroughs, cathedral cities.
Harder to grub out than tree-roots, woody noses
into everything, than dean and chapter.
Instead, scar them with music we daren't face up to:
the Don's descent to hell, a decent set of *Lamentations*.

The Market

after Edward Burra, *The Market* (1967)

Fruit and veg, ink and wash stall: little potato pearls,
pears blanched like white pear blossom,
blessed cabbage blameless embryos, a wallpaper
slapped over shop-fronts, side of a bus, its
windows dressed, sliced, pickled dreams,
ghosts, gherkins, ghoul-packets. The pavement
a slop of lost feet, gargoyle dogs, kid klingons
wild on the top deck. The rest of this universe
lumbered over like cows into a slaughter-truck by
people we never wanted to be, can see through,
through the bone, maybe we were once, forgot how to,
irresolute, the dumbly curious, on our way to a date
in a seventies suit, the forgotten of our shopping lists, the just
before extinction evidence.

In the dead centre one arm
like a Tees tug's hawser, hand like iron hook to grapple
my shore flesh, haul me in, the stallholder, her headscarf
off a Dutch School peasant, her face patched and stitched, my Mrs. Death,
like wormy lettuce, oh colour me in my bloodsucker, my
gross of banana, my flesh-wrestler, my fresh tomorrow,
my tug captain, my great inky aubergine.

Hydroponic

after D.H. Lawrence

Figs grow, ripen in Middlesbrough.
After six thousand years, by bold
strategic thinking, delicate
negotiations, a robust partnership
of key sub-regional agencies
here they are in Nature's World
palace of concrete and polythene
behind the Blue Bell in the bushes
these swollen dusty beetroots
these stallion's testicles gone rusty
these well-hung wonders of the hydroponicum.

Little wonder *Mother-in-Law's Tongue*
has ceased its wagging, gone green
or that a *Cup of Gold Wine* has
spilled down the wall of the hothouse.
Already there are reports of
giant plastic ladybirds
screwed onto tree stumps
where lanky whips of freckled stem
can have their way with them.
The exhibitionists of the plant world
are gathering, rubbery, tattooed intimates
flaunting blossoms like open wounds
pistils of pinky yellow.

Small Eden, free from soil, from weeds,
disease, from all imputation
sheltered from stormy blast, always in the light
temptingly fragile, easily seduced
when poets get their teeth into your figs.

Send for Zero, Hero and Nero
the intolerant ones
send for the Hydroporn Squad
the rays of flashing lights
the superintendent angel. Let them cast out
the grubby-fingered peddlers of verse
on the winds of dispersal, the muddy verges
of dual carriageways. Set up a working party
Figs in the Post-Industrial Economy
while there is still time
and issue protective clothing
to search school book-rooms
for hidden sunburst rhymes.

Horse-on-Tees

Thornaby's giant gull
and Preston's champion crow
hop and swoop,
eye up a Romany horse.

Shaky in the legs,
this Romany horse
and long in tooth,
been chipping away
at this mixed grazing
a hundred years,
fields of crazy concrete,
pastured paving.

Thinking of lying down
on what's left of them fields
and trying on dead for size?
A big mistake to make,
you tired old scrag-end.
No way these birds will consider you
art in a public space,
memorial to your lost race,
heroic licker up of polluted verges.

Meat is what they keep
in their cold stare,
eyeballing both your eyeballs.

After fighting talk, a little booze
and on-the-side
schmoozing beak to beak
with god-knows-who's,
they'd settle on one each,
throw a party after
in a convenient hostelry
with diner, mebbes the Eagle,
for senior associates, partners,
a greasy lawyer to chew.

Better for the rest of us if you
stay weary on your hooves at grass,
let another century pass,
see what the wind blows down
or the Tees shrugs out, what's
cooking on the gas turbines,
when the fair's in town,
who's sorry now.
And your bones won't get
planning permission,
not on this estate,
not on these well-lit roads –
the Council have made that
clear as their Crystal Mark.
Plain as a prairie.

Boro Fan

My friend John's
a Boro fan,
supports the Boro
rain or shine,
win or lose.
He says
someone has to.

It's how you tell
a real supporter.
He'll be there, will John,
fair games, fouls,
good days, bad ones.
He says
someone has to.

Every season
these new signings
with wages bigger
than anyone dreamed of
when John was a boy,
they don't suffer.
He says
someone has to.

Most of them leave,
they get injured, they don't
come back from holidays,
their wives complain,
it's too cold, boring,
they catch the plane, John knows
most of them don't last.
He says
someone has to.

John agrees with them,
it's cold and boring.
They're right, not wrong,
they don't belong,
don't know the song,
haven't put the years in
on the terraces
the thick and thin years.
He says
someone has to.

It's John. He has to.
It's a job for life
being a Boro fan.
He tells me again,
he says
someone has to.

Over the Border

I'm looking for the Customs House
the old one, the way we were
before the transformation.

The river's invisible, licks
along down there, hums its burden
under crane feet, abstractions of the cranium,
glass-and-chrome emporia, o my *Boro Nova*,
an old cat sniffing out to the North Sea,
an old-fashioned stink to it.

Still looking for it, are you, the old one, the Customs House?
It isn't the Riverside, the stadium, all girder legs in a can-can?
Not the Transporter where the cars fly slow, traditional like
cargoes of iron ore, dogs' breath, slave-sweat, Serb girls, soft drugs,
        hard core?
Are you late for a meeting?

He doesn't know it, the Customs House,
he's new like the rest of us,
attacks the taxi he's repairing with a very large hammer,
doesn't know where it or Middlesbrough
or England is, only works here over the border, made it
to a street of car parts, brick caverns, spare dogs. In a white van
two men open their windows waiting for the boatman
who hasn't a clue, might have gone anywhere, if you
enquire at the metal box there, the window, the sign on the door.
        – SECURITASK–

Trail two left legs through puddles, over rust heaps,
by old tyres, could have laid me down, could have cried
my one life, you don't need to read
The Cut-and-Paste Land, the bits you need on a shore are
the ruins, the illegal, the guard dog, the lingo, the raw stuff,
        the rusty sex,
the trespass, the trespass, the forgive us
who are late for our meeting, forgive us.

Oh has it a tower to poke at the clouds, to video the visitors?
You can't see it from here, like.

Metal sheet doorways, plastic blind window shields,
green flickering laughter of mudland where *ex cathedral* stood.
                    – RCIP–

Press the empty button, the enter yard, the gate says, the voice slides
and trips out the Customs House, the old one, the Excise, the Excuse,
the Hack Me Out, the Stab Me In, the new land you found it
all the lines cleared to the drop off the flat world.

Edwin Raymond, Music Maker

Aus Berlin, nicht wahr? But we never heard
that first language. When you left and found this
refuge, this new land, a second *Sprache*
you spoke with mastered emphasis.

You gave a rich return, your flute of flesh,
your spirit's strings, spelled out our shared birthright,
air, light and wings. You turned
our ears to touch, our lips to sight.

So you transformed each changing gummy label
for shifting-sand bureaucracies
to choirs and orchestras,
string quartets, symphonies.

Who will remember you, plain-suited hero?
In Stockton's church your name's engraved in brass,
your song in youth's cascading generations:
Freiheit, Endeavour, the Tees between its gares.

To Geoffrey Sheard, September 2007

I need a bridge through the shifting air
to reach from me to where this arch
of line and colour ends, wherever you are now,
a bridge of sighs, regrets, last words
we never spoke, broken-off projects,
all the stuff that kept us animated when we met,
that keeps me now in this one-sided argument.
You said I had the words in our debates on life and love,
on art and poetry. I use them now, all feathery with breath,
to reach you, if you hear me, with your praise.

Artist and teacher, which do I put first?
Each primed the other, slaked and stoked the other's
thirst, and such a trust between them they'd attack –
and no holds barred – with question, challenge, curiosity,
find satisfaction in this duel – duet – duality of learning.
There go those words again. You taught me reverence,
to see in a young child's marks on paper
the silent burst of understanding, the creator's joy
in this found world. And you showed me
your own marks on paper, how you strived
to catch that world in your net of skill and set it
free, set your soul free with it. By my bed
your *Life Tree* 1978. I wake to it
over the radio chatter of the day and always sense
the universals and the urgency
that pulled the trembling wires of brain, eye, hand,
so often leaving you exhausted and unsatisfied.
While I and others looked on and admired,
you would be off again to find the lost
first makings of the life of earth, the stir
of spirit over the waters, the covenant
of rainbow.

Geoff, before you laugh
and knock me off this cloud of poetry
with some traditional West Riding quip,
it is time I stopped, waved you on your way.
So much I have not touched on.
Let all who knew you have their say, who loved you,
listen to them too. With me, as usual, all words,
shake hands, have a warm hug.
I'll try to say less, see more, learn a little.
At your end of the bridge, leave me a sign,
visual, strong, silent. Meet you in the snug.

For CAK, July 2008

After that last easing out of breath
happened – you weren't wary of it
and I was just a one hour visitor –
I thought so little about it, this was
after all the end. We close a book,
expect no addendum or sequel, it's
too soon to talk about, give a view,
ascribe significance, a long story as
stories go and we got to the last word.
Your face was a woodcut, line and shade,
not a glimpse of fear or victory, just
the dim glitter of ice as you went cold.

Now days have passed with their decencies
you might join those minders in my head
I still make calls to. None that says much
even in dreams, hang around like
old coats by the door, coats of arms
in a dust-locked castle. Try to remember
the phrase, the particular photo, I can
rub, it stays on the page, doesn't light up.
Yet these, with a touch, a weary smile,
wind me to a good day I'll enjoy
different from first time. Can't be sure,
but expect you with a bag of embroidery.

What stories you might rehearse between
my ears. Will it be the same cast of builders,
taciturn men of the moor, children
of old friends who I know and have never met?
And might you complain you have nothing to read,
give your views on the state of the schools?
Thread through needle tellings, still if they're
gladdened by young hopes, reasoned faith,
sorting of strands in freedom's tangle… While out there
the family you drew close-stitched together,
strong-willed, generous, artful, with humbling love,
nurtures your sampler tree, inscribes your long, wise book.

The Shed Door

in memoriam John Savage, 4 February 2007

Early tomorrow in fog and frost
I'll hammer into shed's creaky door
one nail, not tried before, not touched with rust,
from the nail tin in the kitchen drawer.

One nail and enough to remember you with
who sank this morning into the grain,
one and a few heavy blows, as breath
left you the last time. Heavy as iron.

Many a time when I pass the shed
I finger those nails, by smooth and by rough
know and think over the friends who have died.
The hammerer chooses us all soon enough.

Your nail will join them: straight, strong, bright,
telling the timber, while timber lasts,
you proved your metal under hammer's weight.
Early tomorrow then, fog and frost.

For Maggie (Again)

whose e-mail it is that announces
she's put her copy of my book in residence
on the bookshelf of the Nomad Coffeehouse,
Zhongyang Dajie, Jinzhou, Liaoning Province,
The People's Republic of China (now hers)
where it can meet from all over the world
its and her thirsty fellow-travellers.
'Ho Gyan – you've gone global.' I am told.

Visiting you years ago, as remote
as you could get, that far, deep rut of the dale,
I wrote of you plotting a life there, Cote
Bottom. I'm less likely to tackle the trail
to this latest crazy scheme – your words, M. Bede –
but glad you rise with the sun, seeing my poems read.

For a Future Reader

Safe on the shore of your forever city
from fabled books, their wormy memories,
you found and broke my bottled verses open.

You fed the contents, those enjambments
from scribbled time, into the Semios
for instant data-stream analysis.

Before you slip from my long shadow's kiss
I'll shape a guess what harm my poems did
as they translated to your music-thought.

As if you shivered with the cold I'd caught
or harmonized to my life-crackled song
and laughed or wept until you died, corruption

having mined you. Poets without question
should be banished, spell-bound messages
returned unopened. Or you'll lose eternity.

The Light

       rubbing our tired eyes
the light
       diving from the board the slow dive
the light
       abseiling the sky
the light
       writing its next-to-last will
the light
       rendering the hills in its wash
the light
       considering moonlighting
the light
       speechless at what it signifies
the light
       failing for everything
the light
       wanting a bed for the night
the light
       about to deny its name
the light
       not comprehended after all that
the light
       diminuendo
the light
       reduced to a rim, pinned into stars, satellites
the light
       bursting in horizon bubbles
the light
       aquamarine, turquoise, emerald, bruising indigo
the light
       going under for the third time
the light
       asking for a light
the light
       the black page spilling on its words
the light
       from all ill dreams defend our

the light
        leaving for home, leaving home
the light
        roosting in a wing-dark tree
the light
        the hiss of its first day fading and still
the light
        entering the tomb and counting to
the light
        turning perpetual morning

Down

Only the last of the light in puddles,
in wet eyes. Bullocks at metal gates.

The sky's a rush of tattered suits,
gabardines of grey, charcoal, ebony.

Over there America, little silver arrows
pointing the clear nights this way.

Bruises across a dark wall,
brambles with blue-black fruit.

I know to avoid barbed wire,
the sludgy trench, the night challenges.

Then road rolls out these children:
down they come in this mass trespass.

Uninvited they lift to scrutiny
every bright, brittle word I spoke.

Go back, the way I've come,
I sense the village like a face I've kissed

over and over. All its windows closed.
All its bodies alive and asleep.

Round the Houses

where
lives are so much spent
all deliveries come
where
beds lie short of breath
babies are brought home

which
do not think of death
are as safe as selves
which
watch their gardens grow
put weight on their shelves

while
lights switch on and glow
doors open, shut
while
children pack and move
paint pulls on its coat

why
need for so much love
that was so quick to burn
why
we said what we meant
and it turned to stone

Watershed

This road is growing a river,
let out from grassy puddles
it swells the unlined middle,
knowing what's round the bend:

near lift-off, hedge-smacking waves.
It's tidal down there, a road-rage,
a rush-hour waterway
to ripped bridge, jammed junction.

I'm headed up the tops,
where the curtain's drawn tight,
that well-known wipe-out,
mild cloud, Atlantic-thick.

Further predictable stations:
stone-wall tears, rain sniggers,
trickly twists and cambers,
known-to-be-slithery surfaces.

I'm safe as the skyline,
I wield the watershed,
part the sea-strands
this way and that way.

Not a one that can hurt me,
those flooders and drowners,
their cascading snares,
the jaws forced with fishes.

Rain Falling

From the broken spine, the weary, worked-out hills,
my arm reaches to the trampled horizon, unravelling the dale,
thirsting in all its veins, stretched to that hand nailed to the gares,
the towering cranes, ships loading steel, the seals waiting tide's
      turn.

Down from this altar, cloud-wrapt source, inexhaustible weeping
      fell,
the sacrament of red clay flows, the anthem of gathering waters,
the heavens' fractured glass, bruising pools under high foss,
the draining of fields, settlements, factories. The bright cup of the
      sea.

Into the air, launch into the air, buzzard attending the rough high
      grasses,
heron spanning the quiet stretches, cormorant scouring the
      estuary,
hungry for the shiver of movement, the sliver of wet lightning.
My bones and flesh given to their tongues of flame.

Through this high window a distant line of greening trees shades in
my calendar, warmer spring, the wettest summer, my slow hours
grandchildren's birthdays dance through; we rejoice together,
their growing limbs, their love in learning life. May it last forever.

Rain falling to earth, its miracle, its succession of miracles.
A vision we can't comprehend, lacking the languages:
river music, birds of air, fish, seal flesh caressed by dark waters.
Be silent, listen. It is all of us, living and dying.

Spades

The king of spades
looks down on a golden table,
it's his. Everything is, he eyes
his shining reflection
in the golden table, admires
his ermined and embroidered belly,
his short sword, flat and edge
held up and down, his hard and golden hat.

This king has never held a spade,
hasn't driven it down in soil,
his hands are white, his furs are white,
he's never had to scrub
the dirt out of his nails,
delicate oval pearls, slivers of moon.

If he has legs, we aren't allowed
to see them. Feet and private jet
never touch soil. Where did
his fine fibres root, the sheep of his woollens
graze? Where did the winter stoat drag
its belly down to a hard stone, attentive
to prey? Or his hairdresser dispose
trimmings of royal beard?

When his flesh decays, it will be locked in stone,
in gold, in lead, in cedarwood, in silk.
Unsoiled, a proper worm-riddle.
Rich dead bones, safe as a saint's
in jewelled reliquaries, set into altars,
marbled in basilicas the tourists
wash through, tired of treasuries,
weary of granite floors and bright mosaics.

Look at us all, outside and afterwards,
bottoms on palace lawns, shoes off,
toes scratching at crusty clay.
We are sick of your majesty,
all your angelic orders.
We will queue at the ironmongers
again and again, the smell of soil
in our lost souls, the desire for our
garden back, our equality of earth.
We will return without passports,
carrying spades.

Advent

Now I am the Bishop of Somewhere
– some way off and not too important –
but live here with dogs and horses
and folk who know what life is about.
I wear loud sweaters and bark urbanely,
trot round the neighbours' houses
drinking their wine by night. Good to know
that geese still get fat, are even organic
and Christmas is coming with thank God no likelihood
of martyrdoms or pogroms but mince pies and holly
and pedigree conversation in Little Sodden
through which the Roman legions marched,
no angels under the standards of Constantine.

Discovery

On finding there are no saviours, that no faith
though necessary is to be trusted, that
friends' kindness shows them helpless,

when October sun – days before clocks agree
dark nights have come – a failing god, bangs at the window:
Au secours! Oh you suckers! Did you believe me?

Brief, but the colour burned the glass and if
the next day is (it is) grey as an old man's bed
and beard, snatch from the parishes of death

his breath-sucked words, stained snaps of grace
the light touched once enough and stayed
enraptured in a glossy surface.

What there is. Keep it for keeping's sake
with mildewed book, scrapped manuscript,
half a story. Scrape them together, rake.

Don't burn the heap, turn leavings over
to curious offspring timed to poke and weep
at their own singleness, winter's best offering.

At the Parish Church

Words grow together this way, weave themselves
in compound patterns: poet's inky flick
or twining through the generations' tongues.
German can build them gamely *durch Technik*
and genius – as with *Vergissmeinnicht..*

I'm sat on hard-planked pew at Ruth's *Thanksgiving*,
a word to share past lych-gate, obelisk,
break into fragments, dole out hand-to-mouth
across the town she lived a good life in,
morsels of meat for flocks not fed in truth.

I'd have to be the vicar secular,
pizza man, intone at every station:
'Say one loud *Thank you* (those still separate?),
give thanks for anyone who matches you
to act or word of love, human, divine.'

A simple bread of speech, like muffins, crumpets
I carted for my granddad round this market
most of my years ago, fifty, add a few.
Plain flour and water still rise up when warmed:
the miracle of yeasty flesh, baked word.

Such voluntary of people on this earth
would swell the smoke to heaven. Ruth *sei Dank*.
Go well and in good company where you're bound.
The rest of us are kept alive and anxious,
uncertain what you took, what's left behind.

Your parish needs to find – we're far from certain,
the urban planners have no clue – some dawn,
some blinked awake from dereliction's dreaming,
some seriousness, some loyalty, some reason,
happen some loving-kindness, re-creating

in words like this, two-hand-in-hand-come-one,
what counts in such a living, can be built,
discovered, made to work, saved, blessed. Your children,
grand- and great-grand-children sing the burden,
are not-forgetting, make this your thanksgiving.

A Picture of March

Death and the resurrection
will stage the annual show,
massed bands of daffodils,
for the week-end holiday.
> *The blue sea spills*
> *from a broken cry.*

Spring will puzzle the crowds,
juggling miracles, see!
Eggs, rabbits, a sequinned god
sawn in half, and then!
> *The red sun burns*
> *and the knots untie.*

The river will crack the pastures,
a silver whip licking on clay.
The cows parade, abstract canvas
clowns swaying, spraying the ring.
> *The grey mist binds*
> *the wounded sky.*

Everybody will be up there,
prize-winners, hosanna-spenders.
Love will be led out, dance, enjoy
the food and drink of paradise park.
> *The green field dreams*
> *our dreams will die.*

The pageant, having its yearly turn,
passes, leaves only rinds, dried seeds,
the wrappers, rubbers, numbers
from the stained-glass machines.
> *The white flower bends*
> *when you ask it why.*

Where is the need to break open
bad news, in such plain colouring?
A most sharp loss, so young, lost here
where living is full of future play.
The painting-box is closed
in which the child must lie.

Rising

Ending today, the whisky in my glass
replaced the day's colour, scent and taste,
remarked its minutes' unremarkableness:
woodpecker heard and seen, a distant drill, the blast
of TV gunfire round world's bend. Not a trace
of sense made from these rattled parallels.
I sipped the hours' slow-greening field, hedge, trees;
dredged grainy souls from the driftleaved village pool.

A lunging shadow of the risen spring,
the curlew's bent blade ploughs the clays.
Applause from scrambler bikes as lapwings wring
their mops, rehearse the year's nativities.
Easter's church fills to its prompt: 'Risen indeed!'
Is emptied like the tomb is, like my glass is emptied.

Cats in the Alhambra Gardens

Had them swept out, packed downhill with their sun
to one-eyed corner bars, the dust-heap mountains.
Gone, every last human, and the gates locked.

It is good, we are at one with our god
who has set the glitter of his cats
in these most precious jewelled gardens.

Entombed in every day's intensity
we dream the generations' turn of thread
drilling our claw into that fleshy glare.

Our eyes are hooded, bask in faded blue,
we sense the shift to shadow, to the green
between-light, tremble of guitars that wakes us.

We seek our sharp scent out among rose petals,
roughen the skin of waters with dry tongues.
We mind the trafficking of mice and voles.

The thrum of our galaxy shivers down
each taut spine. Could pounce, could crouch a century.
The city's pinned beneath our lunar gaze.

Truly our god is great, is glittering with us,
our eyes his aquamarines, his opals
on the pitch blue velvet of the gardens.

Legacy

To the young men – who all on earth are blowing it
in cars, on bikes, in minibuses, tanks and helicopters
et cetera, you young exploding over one hot planet
care of wheels and tracks, under wings or rotors,
blowing your thoughts and beliefs out, your fertile seeds,
prayer books and hymn sheets and political posters
that lift and drop their feathers of fireweed,
the dust into the dust into the dust –

I leave: my delight in autumn sweeping this churchyard;
a weather-wormed cross, sandstone, sharp by it
bright flowers all grief; words that double the doubt;
each child of mine and each child's child;
words that breathe and outdance me in the warmed air;
the blood's habit surging my heart there and there.

Turbines

When all our kind are gone
from what's then nameless earth
the storms will churn their arms
in this deep-fettered jive.

They'll grind on, celebrate
that they're God's children:
turbines and leggy pylons
in a conga of wiry limbs.

What questions they might ask,
find doubting answers to:
does the wind drive the song?
the song urge on the wind?

And what they are here for
after that fire, that flood,
where they are meant to go,
if there's a better place.

But we won't tell them,
won't care or want to know.
We have set them to dance
a last fling as the juice runs out.

The State of Play

Not much happens
in the state of play,
nothing important anyway.

The end is near
and it's time to start
so here we go on the stroke of the heart.

Nothing matters more
than the team we choose,
the strip we wear, the reds, whites, blues.

It doesn't last long
till the whistle blows
and the final score is nobody knows.

The sun's in the sky,
the sky's in the sea
and the seasons swing on the floodlights' tree.

Who goes up
and who comes down
dances the edge of a spinning coin.

The time of our lives
runs out to a cheer,
the crowds crowd in and nobody's there.

Today is the day,
it's here to stay.
Tomorrow and tomorrow, it's the state of play.

Muse in Spring

Barely a line I write
when you're away
as if I'd died and left you
the cleared earth
not one word to your name.

And then I sense
you entering again
the ambit of my inner
consciousness, the dark
where poems grow.

To warming sun
they rise and bend your way
and name the moment
what it is, first light
when making's everything.

I know you will not stay
where I'm most welcoming
and know the broken learning
of the heart, that brief delight
of blossom on the tree.

This trembles in the wind
that sails you home,
carries your scent ahead.
You move in wordless and I write.
The days grow longer yet.

Near Midnight

Another day that sets out early summer,
its blossom and its warm air's flow,
what we all wish for when the times allow.

Which might be paradise, life's lasting version,
a rich stew (venison?) that extends
the senses past what doctors recommend

for our late years, steadily losing sap,
leaves, already limping along,
old dears sniffed out by dogs' hungers.

But days split more young brains and hearts
than they spill seconds. Pitiless
as those who lead us in our flashbulb blindness.

Listen, we won't hear tonight's music of
bereaved planets, dumb moons in cages,
comets tearing hair. See, nothing assuages.

There is no better day to die on, so much
unfinished, our solidarity with the snuffed-out
long resisted, though we read round about

despair, the unforgivable indulgence still
with no heaven to lose. The hapless universe
wants me as much as roses, foxgloves, cow parsley

which mint its thinginess in re-inventing selves.
Oh I will sleep, being midnight or almost. There's
hope my heart still pumps come morning's tears.

The Sands of Respite

Washed up that shore, we'd want to cling on there
however loud we claimed the opposite
nodding assent to all that urged us bear
the years' accumulating freight
on frailer shoulders, legs held up with sticks
and frames, arm-crutches, painkillers.

At mealtimes we'd discuss the various kicks
delivered since we last had chance to ask
survivors how they were and if the tricks
the physio played on muscles meant their task
of dressing, standing, walking was achieved
or they'd been stranded in the usual fix.

Well, life was given to us to be lived
and after sleep there'd be a bright tomorrow,
if you believed what's said to be believed
by those that had escaped this vale of sorrow
and offered gratitude in verse as lame
as those they left behind, those just arrived.

Staff pinned such pink and flowery rhyme
to notice-boards. Each butterfly
was crucified, the therapeutic game
got played: 'I can't walk'. 'Try'.
And every fall adjusted sweepstake odds
on black eye, cracked rib, broken limb.

Not meant to linger there: the rods
and whips of optimism drove us home
fast as they could, the special squads
were more effective than they'd sometimes seem
and how the dark dream ambulance
purred up and down along our beach of beds.

Till then, without a second glance
at what the future tries to hold and drops,
we'd focus on the daily do's and don'ts,
the present tense that neither starts nor stops,
the short-lived safeties of intensive care,
wrecked fellowship on such gaunt islands.

October

Nights drawing in, our visitors all gone,
and half way round the earth it might be
dawn and spring. But set your face for winter,
the sharp-tongued matron marshalling the yards.

The garden tries it, every live frond fades
where autumn in obsequious uniform
attends to grey and drooping beds,
the dying, the asleep, dark-cheery evergreens.

I see what passes by this box, this window,
a golden leaf swung on one thread of web,
then swept away, the silent night patrols.
First light, a blackbird makes the sparrows jump.

Such details score the hours, invigilate
each waning minute of the year.
Across the wards the shrinking days
scuttle like chaplains between disbeliefs.

What have we done? the wasted roses ask,
their washed-out blossoms shivered in
this last warm westerly. My way
to figure fall, cased, cared for, behind glass.

Closing Down

The world is full of half price sofas,
the universe getting that way. Cliffs of fall,
each hue of leather, fabric of your choice.
Between these mindless mountains, little me
in my wheelchair, doing my little wheelies,
reverse and forward, left and right,
thick pile carpet snags me. Drags me deep,
there is no escape from the showroom monster,
the grinning of the grim, grime-gulping
Drac, which scythes as it bites as it sucks
dust, dead flies, dried blood up, lost screws,
all detritus up, horsehair, human skin flakes, split ends,
life on this planet as we know it is from afternoon TV,
when the programme's not available, when one last blip
and the screen's gone blank.

All of my days I have abhorred this Vacuum,
this cyclonic howling, this baskerville wail,
this ingestion of every other breath,
this repeated monotone of the Reaper's call.

Look, it's the last few days, never to be repeated,
the sale of the millennium, the century, the decade,
the week. We shall inherit the earth
with nothing to pay until we are dead,
when the army of robotic sweepers removes all trace
of our ruins, our straw house.
And never a two-year interest-free tear
for the species we'd worked so hard for, saved so hard for.

I know, I know,
at the closing down of the sun, everything must go.
All of us caught, packed into bags, boxes,
white fish, cheap fireworks, shipped to another planet,
sprayed out like crummy birds' eyes, fingers,
squirting like Catherine wheels,
slithering like mice droppings,

like the souls of our most loyal customers
through ever colder galaxies.
But not yet, I pray you,
my land of lost contents, my lifetime bargains,
hide me in the shadow of your wings,
the detachable, dry-clean shrouds, let me be,
my pale skin, my scored face, my limp limbs, my cracked wheels,
let me have one more turn of the sun, one last chance,
never to be repeated.

Still Life, Autumnal

Once sent, my spaceship camera
circles that distant sphere,
recording each parched detail,
connected with my brainy lens
to zoom in, track across
what is more than abandonment.

All things here look dry
and delicate, sculptured
in what appear as husks
but might prove more resilient
than metals from earth's ores,
than its hardest stones

or are indeed dust waiting on
one touch of absent breath,
one probing fingertip remote
to just disintegrate,
to atomise, to sift
into the barren plain.

Clusters of radar-pods,
spiny deterrent seed-heads,
dropped, unexploded, fluted shells,
and on this dry sea-bed
mines with the stubby thumbs
of pine-coned forest floors.

A fine apprentice piece,
a deathly beauty quite
out of reach, as if the god,
no less, had demonstrated
how he'd learned his craft,
then jumped the universe

to perfect in our close whirl
of air and rock and fire and tree.
The darkening hemisphere
shreds its used leaves, the other half
mints bright new currency
to light this globe of tears.